HAVE YOU SEEN THE WIND?

HAVE YOU SEEN THE WIND?

KATHLEEN CRAWFORD

ILLUSTRATED BY JANE COPE

VICTOR BOOKS

A DIVISION OF SCRIPTURE PRESS PUBLICATIONS INC.
USA CANADA ENGLAND

One night when everybody was tucked in
bed, a strong wind began to blow.
   It whistled down the chimneys.
   It rattled mailboxes.
   It howled through the trees.
   In a little cottage, an old man and an
old woman were trying to sleep.
   The wind blew and blew.

Inside, the tabby cat was curled up in her basket. She heard the rattling and the whistling and the howling.

"It's too bad," she meowed. "How can a cat sleep on a night like this?"

9

The next morning, the cat was very grumpy. "I know," she meowed. "I'll go and find the wind and complain about all the trouble it has caused."

She saw the ripples on the puddles. "The wind is doing that," she thought.

A big dog barked loudly at her.

"What do you want?" he growled.

"Have you seen the wind?" asked the cat.

"No," he barked, "but I could come and help you look for it. Can you see those trees over there, bending and swaying, and losing their leaves? That's where the wind must be."

The cat and the dog walked down the road until they reached the trees.

There was a carpet of leaves on the ground, and more were still falling. A squirrel was scurrying around looking for nuts for her winter store.

"Have you seen the wind?" they asked.

"No, I haven't," she said, "but I could come and help you
look for it. Look over there on the hill. Some children are flying
kites. That's where the wind must be."

So the cat and the dog and the squirrel
went on down the road toward the hill.
Some sheep were grazing nearby.
"Have you seen the wind?" they asked
the sheep.

"No," bleated the sheep nearest to them,
"but I could come and help you look for it.
Look at the clouds moving across the sky.
We could try higher up the hill."

So the cat and the dog and the squirrel
and the sheep climbed to the very top of the
hill. Down in the valley they could see a lake.
The boats were moving very quickly.

"Look how the sails are billowing," said
the sheep. "That's where the wind must be,
down there."

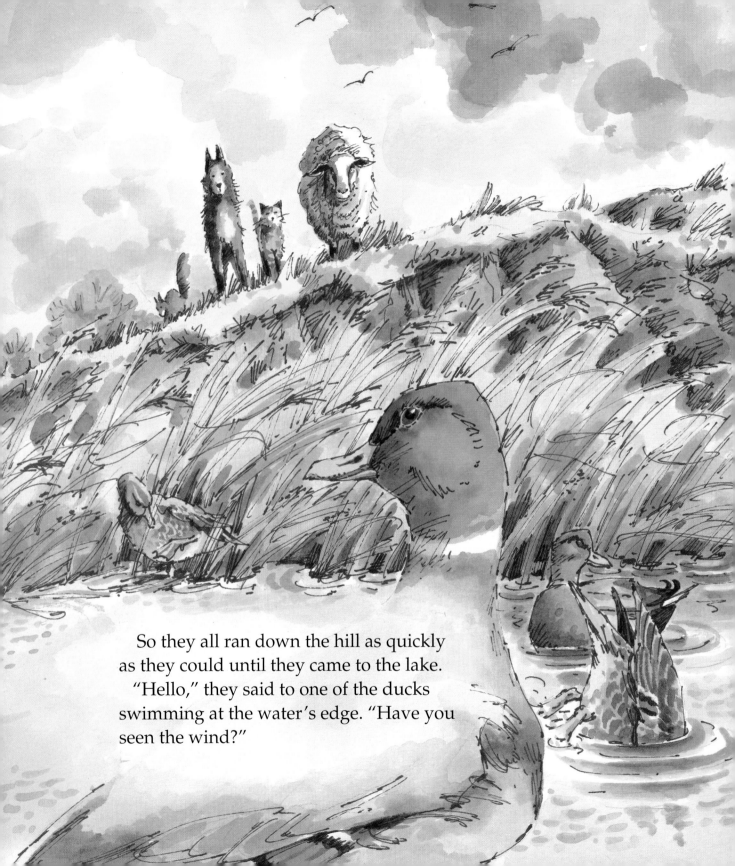

So they all ran down the hill as quickly
as they could until they came to the lake.
"Hello," they said to one of the ducks
swimming at the water's edge. "Have you
seen the wind?"

"I'm afraid not," he quacked, "but I could come and help you look for it. There's a field over there with a scarecrow in it. His hat's just blown away. Perhaps the wind is over there."

So the cat and the dog and the squirrel and the sheep and the duck went into the field. A few bright red poppies were swaying on their fragile stems, and some harvest mice were scampering around at the edge of the field.

"Have you seen the wind?" asked all of the animals.

"No," squeaked the harvest mice, "but in that wood over there is an old oak tree. A wise old owl lives in there and he knows everything. Would you like us to show you?"

"Yes, please," they replied wearily. They had walked a long way.

So the cat and the dog and the squirrel
and the sheep and the duck followed the
harvest mice into the middle of the wood.
High up in a gnarled old oak tree perched
the wise owl.

"Too-wit-too-woo," he hooted. "What
do you want? You're disturbing my sleep."

"Please," said the animals, "have you
seen the wind?"

"We've looked everywhere.
We saw it making ripples on the puddles,
making the trees sway,
blowing leaves on to the ground,
tossing kites into the air,
making the sails on the boats billow.
    It even blew the scarecrow's hat onto
the hedge."

    "And," said the tabby cat, "don't forget
all the noise it made in the night."

The old owl listened patiently.

"Listen," he said. "No one has ever seen the wind. You can hear the noise it makes, you can feel it blowing all around you, and you can see what it does to the trees, the kites and the boats. But only God knows where the wind comes from and where the wind is going. There are some things that only God understands."

"So I cannot see the wind," said the tabby cat, with a sigh.

"Are you sad?" asked the dog.

"No," the tabby cat said thoughtfully, "because now I've learned something new and special about God."

The animals thanked the wise old owl and started the long walk home.

At last the tabby cat reached her cottage.

"Where have you been?" asked the old man and the old woman, giving her a saucer of creamy milk.

She lapped it up, purred, and curled up in her basket by the warm fire where she soon fell fast asleep. She was just too tired to tell them.

"Do you not know? Have you not heard?
The Lord is the everlasting God, the creator of all the world. . .
His understanding is far beyond our own."

(Isaiah 40:28, *paraphrased*)

A Tamarind Book

1995 edition published by Victor Books/SP Publications, Inc.

in association with SU Publishing

130 City Road, London EC1V 2NJ